defining Luxury

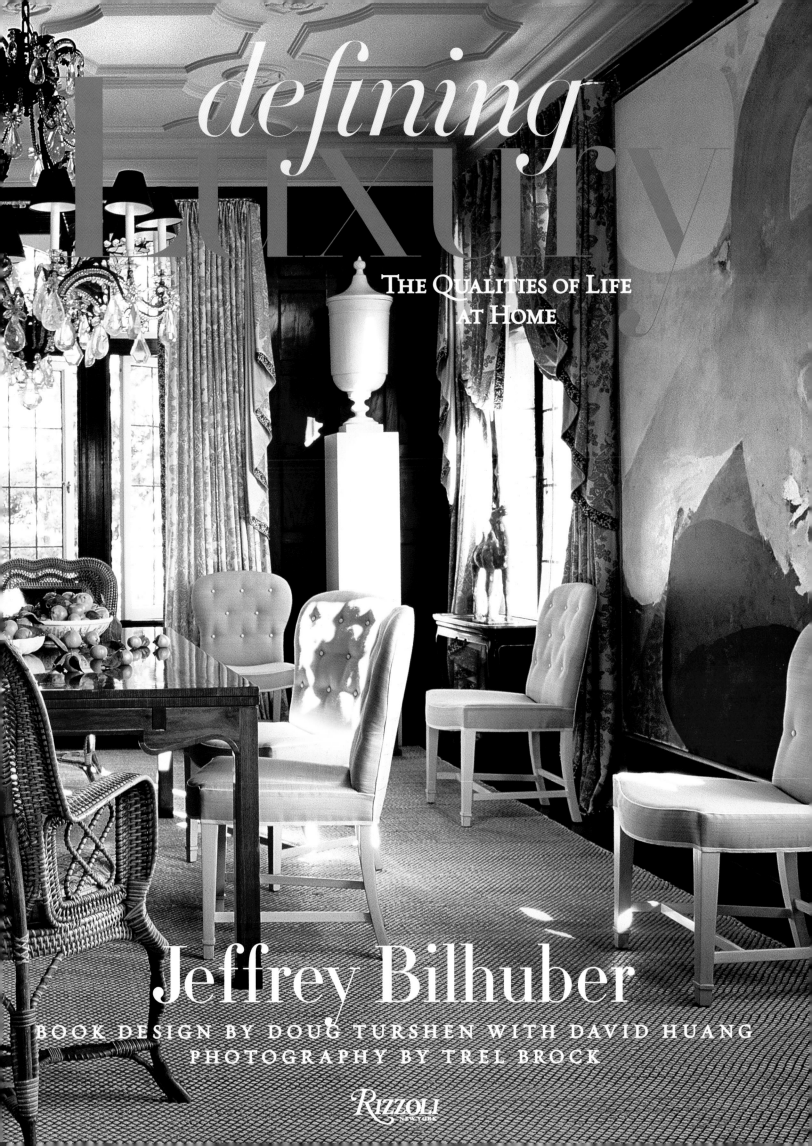

defining
LUXURY

THE QUALITIES OF LIFE
AT HOME

Jeffrey Bilhuber

BOOK DESIGN BY DOUG TURSHEN WITH DAVID HUANG
PHOTOGRAPHY BY TREL BROCK

RIZZOLI
NEW YORK

For
Johann Christoph Bilhuber
2007 –

who thanks

Johann Christopher Bilhuber
1702–1762

*In my son's nursery, a spontaneous mix of well-chosen
colors, patterns, and textures reflects how I see
the creative spirit we all possess. These forms
and materials have the same allure and appeal as any
great toy, bringing out the child in all of us.*

introduction PAGE 8

discovery PAGE 18

ornament PAGE 124

grace PAGE 158

passion PAGE 50

history PAGE 82

comfort PAGE 190

delight PAGE 220

I love luxury.

I AM CONVINCED THAT LUXURY IS PART OF WHAT MAKES US HUMAN, THAT IT brings us pleasure and pride. Luxury isn't opulence, and it's the opposite of vulgarity. It is inspiration and aspiration, something taught, something learned—an evolving appreciation of good, better, best.

Our desire for luxury is innate. It pushes us to strive for improvement and the gratifications that follow. I have always thought that if I worked hard and diligently, I might be able to surround myself with some of the pleasures of life—those luxuries inherent in achievement, enlightenment, and refinement. Growing up, I admired my parents' friends who had, and showed, their own distinctive perspectives through the worlds they created for themselves. I was inspired by those who chose a color other than white to paint their rooms, those who selected furniture or fabrics with real conviction—people who made statements about their individuality through their environments, assertions that revealed a deep sense of confidence and a doorway to their personalities.

My understanding of luxury has evolved over the years. I still believe that luxury is about achievement and expression, but now I find it in a variety of different riches. I think there's a kind of full, complex, deep luxury that comes with experience: as we learn and develop, our ability to discern and appreciate expands. As we broaden our experiences, we understand more profoundly what comfort can and should be. Thus, for me, appreciation, experience, education, and comfort are among life's greatest luxuries—and, yes, so are beautiful furniture, glorious objects, and ravishing rooms.

"The saddest thing I can imagine is to get used to luxury." —CHARLIE CHAPLIN

SURPRISE AND DELIGHT CAN ANIMATE OUR days. I have a dear friend, a former New Yorker, who now lives in Palm Beach. She misses New York terribly, so last fall, when she was in the city, she hightailed it straight to Central Park. There she gathered up a huge bundle of leaves to take back to Florida. Once home, she carpeted her kitchen floor with those gorgeous autumnal leaves. She simply left them there, underfoot, for the next two weeks. Every time she went into the kitchen, she crunched the leaves with glee! She didn't sweep them up until they were dust, absolutely pulverized. To me, that's the most beautiful form of luxury: it's utterly inventive and completely surprising. It was absolutely an indulgence, but not an indulgence purely for indulgence's sake (though that is just fine). This act of total self-expression was luxury as a force of connection, in her case with pleasure longed for and beauty missed. That kind of luxury is gratis —much like the imagination, which is _free_ but most uncommon—and more joyous than almost anything we can buy. The permission to enjoy life in whichever way suits us: what greater luxury is there?

Can that spirit of delight, of spontaneity, of surprise, translate to the longer-lasting elements of décor? Of course. But it's rare, and it requires a great degree of trust in both your instincts and decorator. Rooms that come to life seamlessly yet almost haphazardly, that appear bohemian in sensibility even if they are not bohemian in style, can induce wonder and awe, because they're fanciful, fascinating, free-spirited spaces. They're full of objects that tantalize, objects that, once seen and coveted, are acquired, perhaps on a whim, more often with great knowledge and premeditation. If you revel in that sense of delight, you may actually find yourself living in a much more interesting and varied world, a world of wonderful objects, furnishings, and rooms—each enchanting, each surprising, each with its own story.

"Luxury must be comfortable, otherwise it is not luxury." —COCO CHANEL

IF LUXURY ISN'T COMFORT, THEN WHAT IS IT? Comfort is what fits, what's seamless, what's appropriate for a particular time, a particular client, a particular way of life. As recently as ten years ago, the components of a so-called "luxurious" décor still had a certain formulaic quality. If you were in Santa Barbara, California, it was a hacienda-style house with Mediterranean furniture. Greenwich,

All of the materials in this family room give pleasure to the eye and the hand, so one perceives luxury even before crossing the threshold.

Connecticut, had an eighteenth-century American view with lots of brown furniture and chintz. Palm Beach was all cottons, colors, and bare feet. That's no longer the norm. Today comfort comes from the pleasure of living on your own terms with your own choices in an environment tailored to suit you. My clients are articulate, self-assured, well-educated, creative, and successful families who live very full and rich lives. I want their houses to reflect, support, and encourage that. My goal is to create beautiful, comfortable, deeply personal rooms: to craft houses, apartments, and gardens that honor the pleasure we take in a life well-lived, a life buoyed by curiosity, accomplishment, and family.

Decorators have long been considered great cultural barometers. So we are. Our work reflects changes in lifestyles, in politics, in societal norms and orientations. We express the moods and attitudes of a particular time and place through the elements of design and decoration: materials, furnishings, fabrics, floor coverings, color palettes, lighting, objects, and art. Obviously, our choices should respond to the way that we would like to live and raise our families. But however indulgent, austere, sublime, grand, or modest, the rooms we decorate can and should be of our time. They should live and breathe as we do, with the comforts, pleasures, conveniences, and habits of our particular cultural context, enjoying the very best of the past and optimistically looking toward the future.

"Everyone is dragged on by their favorite pleasure."
—VIRGIL

LUXURY IS DISCOVERY. THE URGE TO LEARN, to seek, to find, and ultimately to acquire is elemental to human nature. The more we know, the richer life becomes and the more discerning our critical eye. Inquisitiveness informs acquisitiveness. Education yields appreciation. Learning to see is a lifelong and deeply rewarding process. The objects of our passions and dreams—Cycladic figures, twentieth-century photography, majolica, pressed glass, first editions, Chippendale furniture, drawings—all have narratives of their own. As we understand their stories and treasure those objects further, as we share our passions and the knowledge they bring us, they enrich our lives: their history makes our own lives deeper and more complex, and vice versa.

Architecture, decoration, and the fine arts are particularly seductive luxuries, as our forebears also realized. Think of those seafaring New Englanders, discovering the Old World while driving the economy of the New. Hunting whales from Africa to the Far East—and returning to dock in New Bedford or Nantucket with lacquer from Japan; ivories and porcelains from China; spices from India; a hold full of oranges from Asia; and pineapples from Brazil. What's more luxurious than the fruit of foreign shores?

Americans have a history of cultural cross-pollination. We accumulate experiences, memories, and objects with terrific zest. We go to Spain and return with hand-hammered ironware. We venture to Asia and bring back lacquer or cinnabar, to Portugal for exotic tiles. We visit France and revel in a set of eighteenth-century gilded furniture. When we're home, we combine our newly acquired treasures with those we already have in rooms made distinctly American by their comforts, from famously luxurious upholstery—which we do better than anyone in the world—to ample and varied lighting to handsomely proportioned, well-tempered atmospheres.

Our pleasures guide us as we move through each day of each year through life. Our eyes, heart, and soul attach us to the gloriously tempting wherever we find ourselves. We're as likely to find something we love in Polynesia as we are in Pennsylvania. It may take energy to seek it out, but it is there—and worth the effort, because good things, great things, last longer, and what we love never goes out of style.

"Take care of the luxuries and the necessities will take care of themselves."
—DOROTHY PARKER

AMERICANS ARE CONSUMERS WITH PURPOSE. What better example of the American capacity for growth through acquisition and interpretation than Thomas Jefferson? Unlike many of the Founding Fathers, Jefferson traveled widely and well—to the world's great courts and cities. Each observation, every experience, found its outlet at Monticello, which exemplifies the American perspective precisely because it absorbs a myriad of influences. Here is one of our country's great houses: a Palladian structure built on a Georgian form with French furniture and English decorative elements, and vast cellars of imported wines—a plenitude of luxurious details, as only an American can bring together. Monticello is America's house, for all its worldliness and luxury of materials, finishes, and forms.

History is a luxury for all of us. Whether on a grand, epic scale or measured in daily or yearly increments, time changes our perspective: in time, we see things with a fresh eye and an objective view. That kind of time is one of the few luxuries that a decorator can encourage, but can't make. What decorators do is create rooms that marry their clients' memories to the present and help them move forward into the future: decorators establish the stage and provide the framework and foundations from which we and our families can grow. In general, houses and their contents improve over time through doing what they are designed to do. It's important to engage in daily living within your rooms, because their beauty grows as they become useful—and used.

Luxury is grace. Grace requires backbone and confidence, rigor, discipline, and precision. It rarely comes easily, and it demands a special kind of economy.

Think of the grace that is the white room, where nuance and subtlety create serenity and intimacy. Clean, enlightened, intelligent rooms are quiet in their variety and full of finesse. They don't shout; they whisper. They converse. Every element contributes to the whole, and every element also stands on its own merits as a sculptural, finished, or material form. The eyes assess and judge: the more you look, the more you see.

"Work is often the father of pleasure." —VOLTAIRE

IN MATTERS OF DECORATION, THE PLEASURE (and therefore the work) often lies in the details. Details require invention. They are specific, individual, and unique, designed and handcrafted by exacting, experienced workrooms and artisans. Great decorators conceive the thousands of details of each room and of the finished house. They assemble and direct the artisans and tradesmen integral to the process, who craft everything with great care, by hand—a faux bois wall treatment, the French knots of hand-loomed linen, the flange on a lumbar pillow, the box pleats of a lamp shade, the hand-forged hardware, the gilding, the plaster, the marquetry, and more.

To create beauty, ornament, and detail takes energy, enthusiasm, refinement, and trust. Think of a set of curtain panels, for example—gloriously appliquéd and hand-embroidered at the hems. From concept to completion, the process takes several stages and dozens of meetings with various people: first sketches, then tissue-paper shells, then cutouts in kraft paper, later the first embroidery sample, and finally the full-scale maquette. Each truly extraordinary detail and form requires care, love, talent, and time. Sometimes the detail that creates the most delight may not be so easy to discern—like the use of handblown glass instead of standard glazing, glass that is imperfect, fragile, but gorgeous. Glass such as this changes the quality of light and the way it moves through space. That kind of nuanced detail can affect the way you feel in a room; it can be more important than other, more obvious indulgences.

"There is no sterner moralist than pleasure." —LORD BYRON

AS AMERICANS, WE ARE A PRACTICAL PEOPLE. For us, luxury begins with function. Yes, Mr. Sullivan, form (even ornamented form, as you knew better than most) does follow function. Pleasure, even delight, results from necessity served: the history of the decorative arts can be one of ever more costly, rare, or beautiful versions of useful objects—for example, a chandelier. Crystal sparkles and catches light: the chandelier is "on" even when it's not, in other words.

The overpainted image of Versailles hanging above the sofa looks utterly contemporary. It's a metaphor for how we resolved the decorative issues of this house.

During the day, the crystals capture light and disperse it around the room. In the evening, those same crystals amplify the light sources (whether incandescent or candle), animating the art of illumination. Function comes first (and last), because if the chandelier doesn't work, if an element of a design is unnecessary, out of place, irrelevant, or simply inappropriate to its surroundings, then it's not worth it. The components of luxury are luxurious not solely because of their value or rarity, but because they perform their jobs well.

We have all learned as Americans that participation is both a privilege and responsibility. What's democracy without choice? Without the promise of options, where's the American dream? It's up to us to cull all of our options, to inform ourselves of their viability, and to make our choice—enlightenment gained and entitlement earned. Certainly the personal is political: every four years we throw the big switch about what matters deeply to us and to our futures. Likewise, the political is personal: we exercise choice every day in matters great and small, from what to eat for dinner to where we vacation to what we wear. We cherish our right to choose for ourselves in every sphere of our lives, public and private. Decoration is the same: it is simply the big switch thrown at home. Because we have the luxury to choose among all the available options, we do. Great decorators help their clients narrow down their choices to those which best express their desires

and aspirations, their personalities and their true selves. These luxuries of choice are those of discovery, passion, history, ornament, grace, comfort, and delight.

Choice is also power. Sometimes we experience that power early in our lives, and often at home. Remember the joy of picking a paint color for a childhood bedroom, or the pattern for the bedspread and the curtains, the thrill of defining our surroundings (and thus ourselves)? Who wouldn't want more of those opportunities and experiences? Thousands of alternatives exist for the choosing, but luxury lies in limiting those thousands to the two or three best—and opting for the one you love most.

There's an old French adage that translates, roughly, as, "If you have a dollar, spend fifty cents on bread and fifty cents for flowers." I'm certain this is absolutely correct. Beauty is necessary, as necessary as bread. We have the responsibility to take care of ourselves and our families, to meet or exceed our basic requirements, but we seek and require beauty, too. How we do that is up to each of us. And what greater luxury do we have than the opportunity of choice? Pick your favorite? Choose what you love most? Fill your life with comfort, pleasure, beauty? We should all aspire to that, at every level we can afford. So spend your fifty cents on bread. But treat yourself to the fifty cents for flowers. Luxury is a necessity, the best possible choice for a life well-lived.

I dream about yellow bed hangings. There's something fantastic about waking up in a golden glow, and I love taking a nap in the embrace of such a perfect color.

discovery

WITH EVERY BREATH, WE EXPERIENCE DISCOVERY. IT'S HUMAN NATURE TO SEEK THE new, to look instinctively for what tomorrow brings, to anticipate our future.

"The art of teaching is the art of assisting discovery."
—MARK VAN DOREN

DISCOVERY TRANSPORTS US. IT IS BOTH A JOURNEY AND A DESTINATION. CURIOSITY often prompts discovery and frequently leads us to the joy of travel, from a voyage across the international date line to an odyssey through the rooms, corridors, and attics of our house. Glorious interiors ensure that the domestic landscape transports us on a daily basis. The finest decorators are brilliant teachers and guides: if we practice our craft at the highest possible level, we open our clients' minds to the luxury of options and the remarkable opportunities these present. The process of exploring those opportunities leads us to discover within what we may not have known existed—an exhilarating and satisfying process.

Decoration is a form of communication, a language of self-revelation. We all want to surround ourselves with what we believe reflects us, to create an environment that expresses our personality, knowledge, and style. Given that, we can refine our vision, our tastes, and our desires. We can always aspire, and we can always educate ourselves further about what matters to us. At best, we can use the elements of décor to help us declare more truthfully and poetically who we

PREVIOUS PAGE: *Intimate artworks, prominently placed, draw the viewer in; a cloth of white monk's wool veils the table's nail-head trim.*
OPPOSITE: *The foundations of a great room can be essentially simple: a handwoven raffia carpet grounds this room's exuberant forms.*

are and what we value. We evolve, and thus communicate more clearly. Whether opulent or modest, brazen or quiet, that decorative language of communication, what I call the dialogue of design, is admirable and essential.

"Discovery consists of seeing what everybody has seen and thinking what nobody has thought."
—ALBERT SZENT-GYÖRGYI

THE URGE TO DISCOVER SEEMS QUINTESSENtially American, from the Pilgrims to today's music and technology pioneers. From our earliest days, luxury—American luxury—has involved the foreign and the far-flung. It must have been fascinating to return to the New World with a fruit, a vegetable, or wine, as our predecessors did. Such discoveries sometimes transformed, even created, traditions in our then-nascent country. How else does a strange fruit become a symbol of hospitality? The Brazilian or West Indian pineapple ends up on the dining room table in New York because the well-to-do wander far enough to find it. In time, the once-novel form of the pineapple is appropriated as a decorative motif—a door knocker, for example. The eventual evolution into a metaphor for hospitality seems only natural. Those with that kind of prosperity shared it in a way that quite literally opened doors to the house, as well as to new cultures and ideas. In Nantucket (as in Boston and elsewhere), affluent families began gilding the lily, as it were, silver-plating the brass pulls, knockers, and knobs of their grand merchant houses lining Main Street. Pride? Indeed. Luxurious? Absolutely. Appropriate? Completely. That's discovery, accomplishment, and polish conveyed through the elements of décor.

Discovery can be contagious in the best possible sense. I once had a client who was curious about twentieth-century photography. After some initial purchases, we confirmed that she had an astonishingly assured and acute eye for the very best of the medium. That was enthralling for both of us. It certainly transformed the design process. As she learned more, a hobby blossomed into a passion—and the project evolved into a stage for her growing collection. From those first few images, she has now assembled a superb anthology of twentieth- and twenty-first-century masters of photography. Discovery informed décor, and now décor defines both self and place.

"The real voyage of discovery consists not in seeking new landscapes but in having new eyes." —MARCEL PROUST

In eighteenth-century France, it was traditional to use one fabric throughout a room to create intimacy, and in the twenty-first century, it's still appropriate and successful.

Decorators can guide clients and their families to an elevated standard of living. At its best, the process is similar to discovering a brilliant museum, one you had never entered before or even knew existed. Once you pass through its doors, your world is forever changed. You may never revisit your old world again. If you do, you'll never see it quite the same way.

That happened to a wonderful young couple, clients of mine. Their parents, then living in London, asked them to find a decorator in New York to combine two apartments and design the resulting interiors. This young couple lived in a strictly modern, minimalist way: they were definitely not looking for a decorator for themselves. Since they lived in the same apartment building as their parents, they acted as intermediaries throughout the project—and they loved it. They could say, "I think Dad will like that. Oh, Mom will love this." They helped us enormously, and the process was enjoyable for all. After we finished their parents' apartment, they confessed that they had visited it numerous times simply to enjoy the atmosphere and to relish the sense of accomplishment from a job well done—a huge surprise, since their parents' taste, goals, and selections were so different from their own.

A few years later, this same young couple purchased an early-twentieth-century town house on the Upper East Side of New York with a hybrid Anglo-Portuguese interior, full of straightforward materials, beautiful craftsmanship, and generous volumes of space. They commissioned us to decorate it. When we started to make our conceptual presentations, I wanted to find some middle ground as I felt they might want to take small steps toward a more traditional vocabulary. I thought I would show them something of the old world and a larger view of the modern, and then we would move forward from there—surprisingly, it proved an unnecessarily cautious approach. They wanted to take giant leaps toward tradition and repeatedly turned away from the suggested modern components. The house we've made now is enormously relaxed and self-assured, a place to raise a family—they'll be at ease there for years to come. They didn't see it coming, nor did I. We happened upon the discovery and the evolution together. That experience has provided them with forward momentum to a renewed comfort and intellectual depth. As their lives proceed, they will continue to progress from this newfound respect for traditionalism, and its particular riches and rewards will inform them as they explore other areas, objects, and pleasures.

Curiosity demands openness and energy. It's much easier to do without both, but I believe we should leave this planet better than when we arrived. Isn't life essentially a process of discovery? We seek. We find. We share. We progress. The process elevates and improves us—and in that, the luxury of great decorating certainly has its role and place.

OPPOSITE: *This nineteenth-century Italian table has a micromosaic, or scagliola, an inlay of hand-cut stone.* FOLLOWING PAGES: *Designed to accommodate an ever-expanding art collection, this room continues to evolve.*

PAGES 28–29: *In such a generously scaled room, intimate groupings create warmth and comfort.* ABOVE: *The doors on this magnificent Japanese lacquered cabinet are designed to hide the drawers.* OPPOSITE: *The owner read every book on these shelves, a sign of a great passion—and a great client.*

PAGE 32: *With the goal of seeing even more of these ravishing early-nineteenth-century japanned bookcases, we hung them high.* PAGE 33: *What's more traditional than a window seat in a bay window? Here, there's a twist: the chairs look out, while the sofa looks in.* PAGE 34: *I adore the graphic effect of ebonized shutters against white-painted woodwork.* PAGE 35: *The mirror behind the carved marble blackamoor looks like a window, and it opens up a new dimension on the wall elevation.* RIGHT: *Painting the brickwork floor white is unexpected—a luxurious solution for a very practical material.*

ABOVE: *The upholstered chair doesn't actually belong in the dining room, but when a house is cohesive and well thought-out, you can interchange its elements spontaneously.*
OPPOSITE: *The woven linen curtains help enhance the light and proportion of this room, two qualities that define it.*

Aligning the cloth on the walls with that on the sofa makes this small room appear much larger.

RIGHT: *This client came with the design direction of "gray," and it helped me discover gray anew. It was a wonderful, almost academic challenge: suddenly, I saw gray everywhere, in everything.* FOLLOWING PAGES: *Pattern and color in joyous abandon fill this room with life.*

The painted screen serves as a window onto another world and an exotic destination of dreams.

ABOVE: *We've always taken great pleasure in working with families; this room is one of our first concerted efforts to incorporate family life into daily living.*
OPPOSITE: *The trapunto quilting on the tangerine tufted chair is one of this room's great details and triumphs.*

passion

PASSION IS COMMITMENT—AND COMMITMENT IS A CONSTANT, NOT A VARIABLE,

in great interiors.

"All humanity is passion; without passion, religion, history, novels, art would be ineffectual."
—HONORÉ DE BALZAC

WHEN MOST PEOPLE ATTEMPT TO DEFINE PASSION IN TERMS OF DÉCOR, THEY ASSIGN

it to a color (claret red, daffodil yellow, indigo blue) or an object (armfuls of

garden roses, eighteenth-century silver)—to something outside of themselves.

That's certainly valid. But for me, passion is first and foremost a feeling that I try

to ignite in my clients: without it, a project may be doomed to fail. It is critically

important for the decorator to spark in the client a deep and passionate connection

to this life well-lived—to the joys we can create with the objects and materials we

select, and to the comforts and pleasures those decisions give our families.

Passion and creativity go hand in glove. Anyone looking for a great decorator

should be looking for a passionate personality. I want my clients to respond to what

I do with delight, wonder, and enthusiasm. I want them wowed! When they are, it's

a reflection of how passionately connected I am to the project and to their desires

and dreams. I'll be as connected as my clients encourage me to be. That's generally

true for every designer, decorator, and architect. If the clients are trusting, if they are

PREVIOUS PAGE: *Given the astonishing craftsmanship of these nineteenth-century Italian gondola chairs, we covered the slip seats in a detailed Fortuny fabric.*
OPPOSITE: *Passion can be hauntingly nuanced, a perception of ethereal beauty.*

engaging and can articulate their intentions clearly, they will help us find the best within ourselves—and, therein, the best for them.

"If passion drives you, let reason hold the reins."
—BENJAMIN FRANKLIN

PASSION REQUIRES CONVICTION, COURAGE, and strength of mind. It takes a special brand of determination to narrow down the endless available options and remain resolute in those choices. Imagine, for example, someone who has a vision for a house that can be distilled into one three-letter word: red. As a designer, I have to ask, "Red what?" That person says, "Well, red everything." "Do you mean red chandeliers?" "Yes." "Red tables?" "Yes." "Red outdoor furniture?" "Yes. Red, red, red." A house devoted to red? Great. It's up to me to deliver the most beautiful, invigorating, triumphant interpretation of that word, not simply the type of red-saturated environment you might readily imagine. And of course, the best thing about a red library is an ice-blue living room!

That single directive, however, suggests so much more than just a preferred color palette. It reveals a sure sense of self, a great will, and an enormous clarity of vision. In a world of options, luxury can be very strict; in fact, it can be all about saying no. Rigor and discipline help with the winnowing process, particularly when repeated editing pares away all but one possibility. That's why I find it so admirable when a client who knows her mind comes to me saying, "I see RED!" In a world of limitless opportunities, it's very reassuring to encounter that rare individual who can distill a vision of a desired life into a single sentence or word.

To know passion is to know luxury. Whatever we are passionate about, we choose emphatically. Decisiveness can be brilliant, as the strong use of color indicates. For every color that shouts, there is one that whispers. Your passion dictates your choice. Committing yourself to something distinctive requires confidence and self-knowledge. All of my clients are accomplished on many levels: as business professionals, as superb mothers and fathers, as capable, inspired creative forces. They have made conscious decisions to define themselves, and as a result have found their particular voices.

"Passion rebuilds the world for the youth. It makes all things alive and significant."
—RALPH WALDO EMERSON

PASSION IS A CONNECTIVE FORCE, IN decoration as in life. Suppose you prefer your rooms lacquered entirely in white. Then you meet someone

When clients collect something as brilliant as these twentieth-century ceramics, it's motivating and heartening.

with an equally distinctive point of view, who has chosen to dwell in a Baroque set of rooms, rooms dark and moody, with deeply saturated colors and ornamentation. You may not bond with those particular stylistic decisions, but you will undoubtedly recognize a kindred spirit, one equally committed to the defining of choice and the expression of personality.

Passion can create luxury. I have a client with a vast book collection. She adores books, surrounds herself with them, couldn't exist without them. Instead of doing the expected—that is, making a book-lined, paneled library—we decided to build the bookcases into the bedroom so that her passion, her books, quite literally enveloped her. The bookcases flank the bed and extend over and behind it. It was a choice that felt daring and a bit nervy—and definitely luxurious.

"The only sin passion can commit is to be joyless."
—DOROTHY L. SAYERS

PASSION BRINGS PLEASURE. IT ENHANCES OUR ability to connect, to communicate, to understand. I am deeply and passionately connected to what I do. I hope that my passion is contagious, so that each project benefits from a shared exuberance and commitment. In life and luxury, there are no passionate bystanders.

RIGHT: *Gorgeous, romantic flowers always contribute to a room's success. We have an orchid grower who cultivates and maintains remarkably exotic plants for us.* FOLLOWING PAGES: *This is one of the sexiest dining rooms in America.*

ABOVE: *Passion and romance go together, as this refined, rustic bedroom proves.* OPPOSITE: *This house is a testimonial to family, as this eighteenth-century secretaire shows.*

The large abstract painting was executed by the client's father. "This is important to us," they said. "As well it should be," I responded.

ABOVE: *A house as sincerely filled with heritage and history as this eighteenth-century Connecticut clapboard needs no further embellishment. Everything we put in it reflects that truth.* OPPOSITE: *There's no such thing as a straight line without a curved line to oppose it: in this modernist barn, the eighteenth-century chair and horn table contrast with the interior's strict geometry.* FOLLOWING PAGES: *The gesso-and-gilded finish on this set of eighteenth-century French fauteuils captures and enhances the natural daylight flooding this sophisticated living room.*

ABOVE AND OPPOSITE: *Ghostlike slipcovers on the chairs and the unexpected light sculpture on the floor create haunting visual poetry.* PAGE 70: *This client's brilliant collection of twentieth-century photography includes a Robert Mapplethorpe that enlivens this room.* PAGE 71: *For this house on Long Island Sound, we wanted to capture the light reflecting off the water.*

PAGES 72-73: *The idea of mandarin orange walls in a beach house at first unnerved the clients, but seeing is believing.* ABOVE: *The severity of the existing stone mantel encouraged me to cover the nineteenth-century chairs loosely.* OPPOSITE: *We chose this spot for the sitting area of the master bedroom because we knew it would get the best morning light.*

ABOVE: *The center table as desk transforms our ideas about what a home office should be.* OPPOSITE: *We discovered these chairs in their unfinished condition at a restoration workroom and decided to keep them exactly that way.*

ABOVE: *These rooms simply couldn't exist without red. It unites the forms and objects in the enfilade that follows.* OPPOSITE: *We purchased this Zajac & Callahan mirror at the Winter Antiques Show in New York, and it drove all other decisions.*

*We didn't want to cover
the windows completely, so
we softened the natural
light by adding a valance.*

history

I'VE ALWAYS BELIEVED THAT WE ARE ONLY AS MODERN AS OUR PAST. AS A DECORATOR, history for me involves the story of the object and the material. Where does a form come from? When does it function best? Did it transform lives? Does it still? What memories are associated with the object? What new memories will it create?

Great decorating requires more than comprehending the narrative of the decorative arts. In decorating, history is also personal: the more information a decorator has about a client, the greater the result of their shared efforts.

"History will be kind to me, for I intend to write it."
—SIR WINSTON CHURCHILL

AMERICANS EMBRACE HISTORY CAREFULLY AND CREATIVELY. WE PUT OUR OWN SPIN on what tantalizes us from other times and places. In a recently completed project in San Francisco, I found myself enthralled with the period from about 1848 to 1855, the Gold Rush years and the generations immediately after. As the Gold Rush hit its stride and in the years before the century turned, Americans began flexing their economic muscle. They traveled to England, France, Italy, the Far East, and Russia, where they learned about furniture, forms, ornament, and materials not their own. Once home, they commissioned craftsmen to interpret what they had discovered abroad—thus a surfeit of grandly exuberant French-influenced rooms, English-inspired rooms of baronial stateliness, and opulent Russian-style rooms.

PREVIOUS PAGE: *Swag and jabot curtains clearly refer to shapes and forms associated with history.* OPPOSITE: *To see tufting is to see history: nineteenth-century chair frames were made of metal, and master upholsterers used tufting to create structure and add comfort.*

Ethereal light from this San Francisco house's skylit central core bathes a sofa fitted into the stairwell apse.

"It takes an endless amount of history to make even a little tradition." —HENRY JAMES

AMERICA'S FINISHED ROOMS REVERBERATE with a clear-headed optimism precisely because we reinterpret European decorative devices and architectural motifs to suit our particular times and tastes. Hence our nineteenth- and twentieth-century interiors with such imported influences as ebonized panels with French revivalist forms wed to cloisonné inserts and bronze dore mounts—forms European in origin, but American in fact. The brazenness to marry such diverse traditions makes us uniquely who we are. That's what is so compelling about the character of the Unsinkable Molly Brown. We can be exuberant and refined simultaneously. We can keep our gingham crinolines underneath our fancy ball dresses. We may travel to Europe and the Far East, but we return home and enjoy a raucous barn dance.

Houses, too, often have rich stories of their own to tell. So many eighteenth-, nineteenth- and early twentieth-century houses along the East Coast began as clusters of farm structures, each with their distinct purpose. If the property prospered, the farmer expanded and merged the individual outbuildings into one grand manse. Those that have survived often remain rooted to the original footprint, a testimonial to the prosperity that America's farmland generated, to the success that our forefathers enjoyed, and to the way they announced their place within the village or town, city or nation, and society as a whole. These houses express the aspirations of their times and, of course, allude to the lives and histories of the people who occupied them.

Interiors can be similarly revelatory. Imagine a client has had numerous houses, each well-loved, inhabited, and, eventually, allocated to memory. Over the years, that client may have amassed and stored quantities of furniture and objects with great personality or sentimental value. Eventually, they find the ideal house to make their own. With warehouses bursting from the previous residences, the client decides, quite understandably, to use it or lose it—Italian, Chinese, French, Continental, Moroccan, and American, low country to high. Both the project and I will benefit from having to work with this constraint. The client has always loved or been charmed by this furniture, and therein lies its value.

"I like the dreams of the future better than the history of the past." —THOMAS JEFFERSON

The tufts peeking through the chair backs are my pun on the "stuffing coming out."

GREAT DECORATION SHOULD HELP US MARRY our memories to our present and move us forward into the future. I always have this in mind when I cull my clients' purchases and possessions. Suppose, for example, a family art collection includes many large paintings done by a brother or a grandfather, paintings that have often been stored in the attic, like some aunt's dreadful wedding gift. If a relative made something, the accepted view is that it lacks merit. On the contrary: it has a deeper significance. All it may need by way of improvement is a snappy frame, a bit of polish, or a place of prominence.

Knowledge is a luxury available to us all. We see the world differently when we understand that objects, forms, and finishes exist for a reason and serve a specific purpose. Why, for example, is a particular type of arm called a shepherd's crook, a saddle arm, or a ram's horn? Look at the shapes and you'll see how each refers to a familiar form. Why does an English window seat, or settee, have a flat outside back and, often, a curved or bowed front? That window seat often rested on the mezzanine landing of the staircase, just at the point where the staircase turned. To avoid catching the corner of the settee on the square edge, furniture makers created a radius across the face. The flat outside back gave

extra comfort to a location of limited depth. The social history of architecture, furniture, and the decorative arts is fascinating and full of wonderful tales.

> *"Civilization is a movement and not a condition, a voyage and not a harbor."*
> —ARNOLD J. TOYNBEE

TO HONOR THE PAST IN DECORATIVE TERMS does not mean to re-create it. We shouldn't yearn for another time or place. No one today actually wants to live in eighteenth-century France or nineteenth-century Russia; life was complicated, dirty, and frustrating, however many extraordinarily refined and beautiful pieces of furniture, fabrics, and objects those eighteenth- and nineteenth-century citizens created for their palaces, houses, and rooms that remain with us today. Be thankful that we now enjoy the privilege of culling ideas and objects from all great ages and cultures and incorporating them into our lives, with all our modern conveniences and comforts, as we move ever optimistically forward.

OPPOSITE: *I believe our interiors should reflect the times in which we live. This magnificent painting by Cecily Brown expresses current trends in art; tomorrow, it will be a point of reference for today.*
PAGES 92-93: *The paneling, plasterwork, and architecture are original in this 1906 house, but the room is fresh and modern in spirit.*

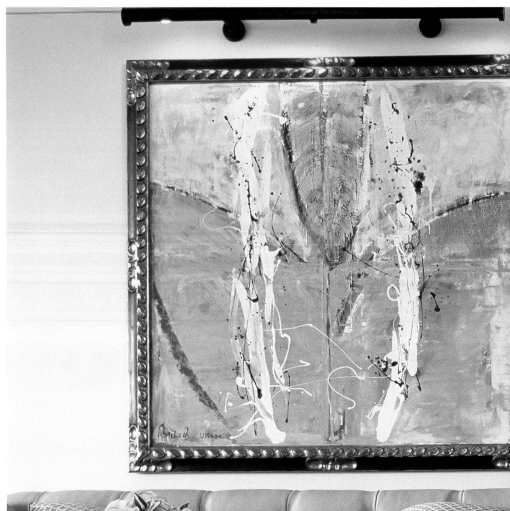

PAGE 94: *Drum tables were created specifically for libraries. I've used this one as a catchall and centerpiece.* PAGE 95: *The stained and stenciled floor creates a sense of expansiveness and alludes to elements found in larger residences.* RIGHT: *Ostrich upholstery shows off the form of these nineteenth-century French Renaissance Revival chairs.* FOLLOWING LEFT PAGE: *I love japanning because the abalone and mother-of-pearl inlays are fascinating, luxurious materials that capture light and animate the surface.* FOLLOWING RIGHT PAGE: *One of four very rare nineteenth-century wicker chairs with an inset japanned panel which were probably made in Sicily for the European market.*

This parlor is deeply nuanced and speaks volumes about history, grand and personal.

ABOVE: *A heroically scaled antique newel garden ornament comes inside, as art.* OPPOSITE: *Whether it's Delft or Chinese, blue and white is history— and it's ravishing with citron-colored walls.*

*Hand-painted de Gournay
scenic wallpapers have created
atmosphere for centuries.*

A Japanese lacquered chest, an inlaid Syrian bench, and an English Arts and Crafts chair contribute to a room with a global view.

*The owners' collection of
National Geographic
magazines makes me feel like
I'm ten years old again,
a boy discovering the world.*

ABOVE: *To find the hues that spoke of history in this eighteenth-century Connecticut house, we gray-washed the floors and scrubbed the walls.* OPPOSITE: *The entry hall's lichen-painted staircase amplifies the handsome architecture and the house's natural light.*

PREVIOUS PAGES: *After we stripped all of the woodwork, we added only painted furniture to introduce color and contrast.*
RIGHT: *If you use a patterned fabric for the curtains, you should always use that same pattern on at least one other piece of furniture in the room.*

RIGHT: *What's more romantic than a library by the sea? In this Nantucket study, with its historic prints and paintings, you can smell the salt air.* FOLLOWING PAGES: *The chairs and tabourets we purchased at Christie's in Paris are 1940s reinterpretations of classic eighteenth-century forms. The eighteenth-century faux-marbre obelisks are from Sentimento Antiques in New York City.*

RIGHT: *It's wonderful that the children of this house use the dining room table for crafts and art projects.* FOLLOWING PAGES: *The romance of this room breathes history: the shared history of family life.*

ornament

I ADORE ORNAMENT, EMBELLISHMENT, AND THE FLOURISH OF DETAILS. I HAVE learned from experience, and fashion, that details can define a work. Whether casual or formal—turtleneck or tails—details succeed through clarity of thought, insight into design, and masterful craftsmanship.

"The details are not the details. They make the design."
—CHARLES EAMES

THE PORCELAIN LIGHT SOCKET, FOR EXAMPLE, IS ONE OF THE MOST BEAUTIFUL objects ever made—a perfect design, one that requires no improvement. As an object, of course, it's a relatively simple, unadulterated form. Yet the beauty of that light socket still depends on a certain level of craftsmanship and embellishment; in this case, embellishment is actually the editing process that streamlines the object, stripping it down to its essence.

Ornament more commonly works the opposite way, that is, as addition. From the dawn of civilization, man has embellished the surfaces that surround him with such forms as calligraphy, or glistening materials like mica, silver, or semi-precious stones. Carving and overlays are further means of adorning, enlivening, and articulating a surface. Appliqué is another option with a galaxy of possibilities. Just think of upholstery: the encyclopedia of applied details

PREVIOUS PAGE: *The lyrical painting by Ryan McGinness is a perfect complement to a banquette upholstered in Fortuny cotton.* OPPOSITE: *The horn-and-silver cups on the mantel give this large, handsome room its scale and intimacy.*

includes cording, contrast welting, strapwork, trims of all types, and nail-head finishes. There's tufting of all kinds and a myriad of fringes—indeed, an entire civilization's worth of passementerie. There are pleats and tucks, folds and flanges. All of these details are admirable embellishments. They typify the best of their craft. What great decorators look for is excellence in every detail, in each ornament and embellishment, from the simplest to the most glamorous or grand.

Perception is a matter of presentation. What looks genuinely lavish may, in fact, be something other. Objects, furniture, materials, and forms don't have to be "original" or antique to be luxurious. There are times when I prefer to embrace the interpretation rather than slavishly admiring the original.

A sleight of hand or a trick of the eye—such as trompe l'oeil murals or painted finishes, from faux marbres to faux bois—are brilliant techniques for adding a human touch to rooms of luxury. Can a great decorator conjure the illusion of limitless space and light in a myopic New York apartment? Absolutely! With the help of some strategic ornament and well-placed mirrors, we can create an enfilade and add a sense of endless rooms repeating to infinity. Might a great decorator or a savvy host refresh a waning arrangement of cut flowers from the gardens with strategically placed artificial blooms? Mixing silk blossoms with garden roses, as the English often do in the grandest of country seats, is a triumph of ornament and practicality.

"I believe the right question to ask, respecting all ornament, is simply this: was it done with enjoyment, was the carver happy while he was about it?"
—JOHN RUSKIN

MATERIALS MATTER. WE CAN ALL AGREE THAT in some way, the more luxurious, the better. We've all seen craft and inspiration transform something plain into something sublime. Even everyday fibers and fabrics such as cotton, felt, and twine can become art, and fantastic ornament, in the gifted hands of the experienced artisan. A wood floor painted in a classic marquetry pattern, contrasting gimp tape on a sofa, mattress cushions with scorched bamboo handles that slide underneath a table, a curtain with a scalloped finish, contrast saddle-stitching on linens, a French flange on a pillow, hand-embroidered monograms: each detail adds a layer of personality and intimacy to a room.

You must train your eye to see detail. Sometimes it's quite affordable, other times less so. It can be obvious in its flourish, or, like the subtle perfection of great tailoring, it can be precise, crisp, and fitted. It can be a lamp shade that helps establish a mood and enhances the room's overall beauty.

Hand-looped gimp on the base of this spoonback chair adds a romantic flourish.

Consider the luxury of slipcovers, hand-fitted and crafted for every piece of upholstery in a house. Creating such a nuanced extravagance begins with exceptional craftspeople, who cut every slipcover in tissue paper on site, the way a dressmaker cuts a form. They then pin the individual pattern onto the furniture, modify, and remove it. Then, it's back to the workroom to cut the forms in fabric, another fitting, additional modifications, and, eventually, a final fitting on the body of the furniture. It's an astonishing craft: however casual in initial appearance, it can elevate the luxury of any room, whether in a beach house or penthouse.

"The key thing is seeing everything grow, setting out with a small sketch and seeing the whole and the details spring to life."
—ARNE JACOBSEN

ONE OF THE GREAT LUXURIES OF THE DECOR-ATOR'S LIFE IS THE OPPORTUNITY TO WORK WITH EXTRAORDINARY ARTISANS, TO DISCOVER AND DEVELOP THE TALENTS OF GIFTED CRAFTSPEOPLE, FROM THE DECORATIVE PAINTER AND THE UPHOLSTERER TO THE HARDWARE MAKER AND THE GLASSBLOWER. HARD WORK AND DILIGENCE ARE NECESSARY to create luxury. One of my greatest pleasures is being in the workrooms on a Saturday morning alongside the cutters, steamers, and seamstresses. On those mornings, we build, shape, and craft beauty, developing it from idea to completed object. There I am, with a mouthful of pins, at the cutting table laying out cloth. I might realize, for example, that just because a particular fabric has a twenty-four-inch repeat with a floral bouquet doesn't mean that the bouquet must always occupy the front and center of the seat and back cushions. It might be more effective hidden in the corner, with a heightened emphasis on the surrounding ground. At that point, it doesn't cost any more to move the pattern around. With the expertise of craftsmen, dreamers, and image makers, we proceed to elevate the designs to a higher level of luxury, one that deeply engages the creative process.

Herein lies another true luxury of decoration. Great decorators know what it means to handcraft from beginning to end, engaging in the embellishments and ornament. They are actively involved in each decision. Each element can be made by hand, to measure and to order, specifically to suit a client and an environment. The options and opportunities are endless. What makes the process luxurious is the chance we have together to define our options—and select those we love most.

OPPOSITE: *The curtain fabric is called Lace, and you can see why. The contrasting tape trim is made of glass beads with metallic thread.* PAGES 132–33: *These curtains are known as Empire or Theater style because they're held back and open like those on a stage. Note how the stripes of the swag and jabot align with the curtain panels, a sure sign of a master craftsman's work.*

PAGES 134–35: *This room is an illusion, with the pattern from the curtain panels painted directly onto the bookcases and shelves.* RIGHT: *This hand-painted scenic wall covering of blossoming almond trees changes color over the course of the day. We went through several generations of drawings to achieve this magical effect.* PAGES 138–39: *Here's ornament as form: the gourd-shaped ottoman designed by Jacques Grange complements the tufted king chair and the slipper chair's scalloped base.* PAGE 140: *Because these portieres are seen from two directions, both sides are finished and trimmed in a contrast tape.* PAGE 141: *Natural vegetable dyes contribute nuances in the weave of this cloth creating subtle variations in color.*

SALLY MANN   DEEP SOUTH
Walda Pairon

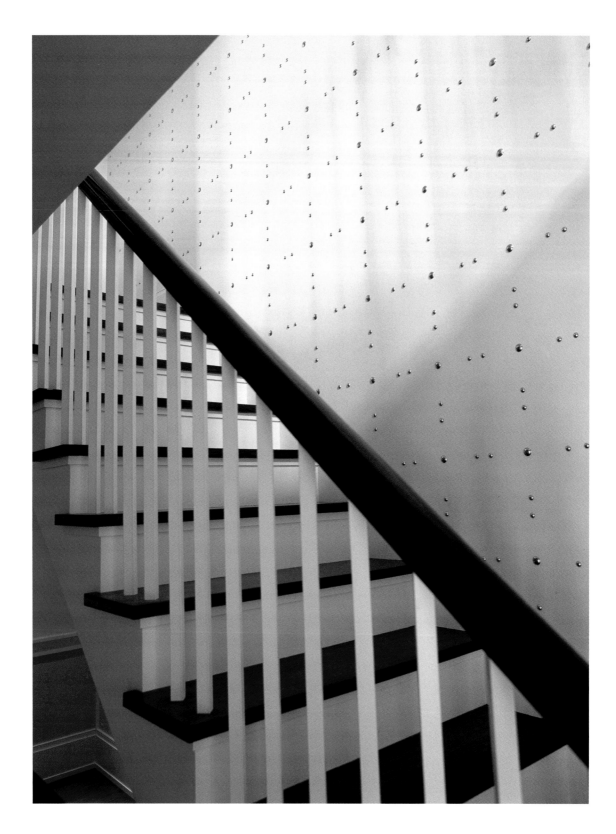

ABOVE: *In this Nantucket stair hall, nickel-plated nail heads are hand-applied to the walls to capture and animate the natural light.*
OPPOSITE: *The ebonized, open-arm chair has wonderful pen-work detail. The pattern is scratched through the finish and then waxed.*
PAGES 144–45: *Ornament compressed, like this room's diminutive Dutch chandelier, assists our understanding of scale.*

PAGE 146: *In Negoro lacquer three different colors are applied, layer after layer, and are then sanded by hand to reveal different hues.* PAGE 147: *The late-eighteenth-century French settee has hand-carved garlands and bouquets, perfect for a woman's sitting room.* ABOVE: *These sconces are from the client's collection; the combination of candlelight and electric light is poetic.* OPPOSITE: *This crystal chandelier captures and moves light through the interior.*

ABOVE AND OPPOSITE: *Color and ornament are
sometimes inseparable. The red Venetian glass chandelier
hangs over a studded lacquered leather center table.*

ABOVE AND OPPOSITE: *This client's breathtakingly
beautiful collection of English majolica is
enough ornament to carry the entire room.*

A Greek mattress, like one on this banquette, must be stitched by hand with a curved needle to hold the batting in place.

ABOVE AND OPPOSITE: *The carpet in this room combines wool and silk in a design based on an Edwardian precedent. The silk pattern reflects the light; the field is matte wool for depth and contrast. On the bed is a natural black velvet chinchilla blanket from Dennis Basso.*

grace

GRACE IS LEARNED. IN DESIGN AND DECORATION, GRACE IS INTELLIGENCE EXPRESSED through form and material. Happily, luxury exposes us to the most refined resolutions of form and function.

"Beauty without grace is the hook without the bait."
—RALPH WALDO EMERSON

GREAT ARCHITECTURE AND DECORATION HAVE ALWAYS BEEN AMONG HUMANITY'S most powerful tools for exploring and expressing ideas about grace and refinement. Grace can, in fact, begin with great architecture, which gets the "bones" of the room just right. True luxury for the decorator is when the architecture sets the stage with rooms that work as well bare as they do dressed. There is no greater challenge for a decorator than having to camouflage or compensate for bad architecture. Conversely, there's no greater pleasure than a collaborative, call-and-response relationship with an architect—one that begins in a project's infancy and develops, as does the project, with gracefulness and purpose.

Grace is a kind of inevitability. It occurs when architecture and decoration are fully and completely integrated—when every component of the house is designed, built, and included into the decorative resolution. Grace is also nuance, from the largest to the smallest detail: seamless poured-plaster moldings that enhance shadow and light, perfectly counterweighted doors that swing open to

PREVIOUS PAGE: *We added this Hudson River School mirror because of its monumental scale, patina, and aura of history.*
OPPOSITE: *What's more inviting on a sofa than a cotton, cashmere, or mohair throw? It brings a welcome touch of comfort to any room.*

the touch, paneling details resolved with nail-head trim instead of the expected field panels—all expressions of the harmonious relationship between artist and craftsman.

Excellence attracts me. I believe American grace reached one of its zeniths in the early nineteenth century with the architecture of democracy—the Greek Revival style, with its deep-rooted foundations in the classical orders. But whether we're discussing Shaker furniture or Regency style, Egyptian or Greek Revival, we're studying creative responses to the functional needs of a particular time, place, and way of life. Architecture and furniture reflect the requirements of specific times and distinct cultures, issues of function resolved through scale, materials, and form. A design is Federal, Regency, Baroque, Renaissance, Rococo, or Italianate because it derives from a particular historical context, from a certain period or place and the needs of its people.

"Will is to grace as the horse is to the rider."
—SAINT AUGUSTINE

I LOVE THE IDEA THAT FORM IS SUBJECT TO translation in the hand of the interpreter and the revivalist, of the craftsperson who is carving, painting, gilding, or finishing the furniture and interiors. For me, Moorish architecture is a perfect example of design's wonderful powers of appropriation and reinterpretation. The Moors were nomadic. As they infiltrated different cultures, they absorbed various aspects of those civilizations into their own. Their architecture incorporates Spanish forms, Romanesque shapes, African influences. The Greek Revival (like other revival movements) is similarly interpretative: instead of creating line-for-line reproductions, the nineteenth-century designers absorbed ancient Greek and Neoclassical ideas of order, intelligence, and democracy into a format to suit their own times and needs. The Postmodernism of the 1980s is a more recent example of contemporary reflections on an earlier architectural movement. Was it successful? History will judge. But success or failure, it was nevertheless an attempt to conjure the very best of our history in a contemporary idiom.

I quite like the word "essential," and I believe that graceful rooms are rooms in which all of the components matter—rooms where everything is vital, rooms that need nothing more and nothing less, rooms where the whole is better than the sum of its parts. In enlightened, intelligent rooms—those filled with a certain grace—each element stands on its own merits but is better because of the objects that surround it. Every material, each form, all of the furniture and their respective surfaces, complement one another

I think it's both kind and intelligent to create children's rooms that anticipate the adult to come, as this young lady's bedroom does. When you do, you raise their expectations of what's possible.

and provide a seamless whole. Rooms such as these are harmonious, inviting, and, indeed, essential.

"I want, of course, peace, grace, and beauty. How do you do that? You work for it."
—STUDS TERKEL

IT'S CRITICAL TO REMEMBER THAT WHEN WE hold beautiful objects in our hands, we are privileged to do so. Likewise, the opportunity to share these objects with others is a gift worthy of acknowledgment. Objects survive us. They go to the next house or to another collector. They pass, like time, through our hands. It's up to us to make all that we can of them, to learn from them, and to improve with what knowledge they give us. Surround yourself with riches, choose them carefully—and care for them well.

Gloriously happy, beautifully turned-out family houses are wonderful places. I'll never deny anyone the opportunity to have more rooms than they can use or have purpose for. Many times, it is justification in and of itself that rooms can exist simply to provide beauty and pleasure. But oftentimes restraint is grace. And intimacy can be a greater luxury than vastness. Great decorators use the grace notes of detail to create a sense of intimacy—to form pockets of warmth, beauty, and comfort in rooms large or small, to transform a house in a way that makes it welcoming and human.

Grace is subtlety and nuance. In decorating, that might mean a palette of neutrals, a composition of white, ivory, beige, and sand. Neutrals reveal form at its most sculptural and show off shape as it is, without the distractions of color and pattern. Great decorators understand the rigor and the discipline necessary to achieve subtlety: materials and finishes become even more important because they're what you see first and last. In rooms where nuances abound, one can focus on the essential qualities of each element and, from there, begin to understand form.

"Grace has been defined as the outward expression of the inward harmony of the soul."
—WILLIAM HAZLITT

EVERY GREAT DECORATOR HELPS SHAPE THE environment clients inhabit. There's so much more to decorating than selecting and arranging objects in space. We feel it when we walk into a room that is refined, a room with a syllabus of indulgence and a vocabulary that expresses our soul and what we want others to know about us. Why not speak with dignity and grace, through spoken word or through the objects, furniture, and architecture that surround us? It's very easy to amass the trappings of a luxurious life, but a luxurious life they do not make. Grace is the urge to create a better, more harmonious, more nuanced place for ourselves and, especially, for those we love.

Hospitality is sometimes as simple as a beautiful bowl of fruit and a glorious vase of freshly cut flowers from the garden.

RIGHT: *A back-to-back sofa is a graceful form that adds intimacy to a room. Here, one side faces the fireplace, the room's convivial heart, while the other focuses on the window and the view beyond.*
PAGES 168–69: *The pair of Jansen mid-century steel-and-brass cigarette tables flanking the client's own settee are from Liz O'Brien Gallery in New York City.*
PAGE 170: *We placed this chair in this spot specifically to capture the afternoon light.*
PAGE 171: *The hot-rolled, mirrored-glass wall panels have an old-world quality; they create a mottled and rippled reflection that softens the light.*

On the book spines:

ARCHITECTURE of the OLD SOUTH

French Scenic Wallpaper 1795-1865

To welcome guests to the entrance hall of this Nantucket house, we built a shaped banquette rather than the more expected center table.

ABOVE: *I use curved-back settees on almost every project because I find the form so embracing and civilized.* OPPOSITE: *The scale of this room is graceful, and the low lamp on the table offers a soothing, intimate invitation to sit and enjoy.* FOLLOWING PAGES: *This dining room is defined by great refinement and liveliness.*

ABOVE: *The eighteenth-century French wing chair is the client's own. We found that it was a surprisingly good fit in this Connecticut clapboard house.* OPPOSITE: *In a house built to entertain friends and family, this room is a grand gesture of grace and hospitality.*

The carpet is shaped like a fanciful giant lily pad, and it encourages everyone to step in and join the group at play.

RIGHT: *Nantucket entrance halls are often austere, but this one is fully furnished so that comfort and hospitality are understood from the very first steps across the threshold.*
PAGE 184: *For me, family silver is a touchstone of elegance, beauty, and utility. This eighteenth-century Georgian silver is used on a daily basis.*
PAGE 185: *From my great aunt's map of America to my grandfather's arrowhead collection, everything in my own dining room has a family connection.*
PAGE 186: *A tea table's scale adds to the atmosphere of conviviality—it asks you to draw up your chairs.*
PAGE 187: *I love romantic bedrooms, as do all of my clients, both male and female.*

From the strapwork on the ceiling to the contrasting tape trim on the upholstered chairs, this room finds grace in the disciplined line.

comfort

THERE IS NO LUXURY WITHOUT COMFORT. COMFORT IS NOT SOME STATE THAT exists naturally; it must be created. Once it is, it embraces us as we embrace it.

"There is nothing like staying at home for real comfort."
—JANE AUSTEN

COMFORT MEANS SOMETHING DIFFERENT TO EACH OF US. IN DECORATION, HOWEVER, we tend to think of it more specifically in terms of upholstery. There are clients who desire luxuriously deep sofas, sofas that are very soft and enveloping. These are sofas that give way to the sitter, that welcome those of us who want to sink into a hug, that encourage us to stretch out languorously, to nestle in for a delicious nap in the afternoon. At the other end of the spectrum are the clients who find the epitome of comfort in a beautifully proportioned upright chair, a chair framed perfectly for the reader, with arm pads specifically designed to accommodate the sitter's elbows when holding a book; small side panels, or wings, angled to deflect the glare of lamp light; and adjustable, or "ratcheted," backs. Each preference has merit and reason: there is a logic to luxury.

Comfort actually involves a wide range of variables. This is especially true of seating and upholstery: each piece performs an individual task, and we make our choices based on both function and form. We're always exploring comfort and its different degrees, because the amount of cushion and the extent of embrace

PREVIOUS PAGE: *The tufted-back settee is one of a pair flanking the fireplace. I think it's essential to build in multiple opportunities for comfort in every room.* OPPOSITE: *This back-to-back sofa is used in a very up-to-date way. Instead of facing the fireplace, one side faces the pool and the other faces inward, toward the living room.*

should be what feels right for the individual. Do you want your mattress to have the same level of support and resistance as your sofa does? I don't. Others do. That's where design comes in: we have various criteria for different furnishings because our bodies require different levels of comfort for distinct purposes. We adjust or alter the scale of comfort to suit—and often make it to order.

"Consider any individual at any period of his life, and you will always find him preoccupied with fresh plans to increase his comfort."
—ALEXIS DE TOCQUEVILLE

COMFORT BEGINS WITH CRAFTSMANSHIP, especially with upholstered or soft furnishings. Many of the world's greatest workrooms are in New York, particularly those that actually construct upholstered furniture by hand. Upholstery making is a true art form and a craft of particular skills handed down by generations of highly trained artisans. Its many stages include cutting the frames from clear, kiln-dried wood; selecting, setting, and tying the springs; determining the most suitable filling (feathers, goose down, wool, or horsehair) for the body; draping and tailoring the cloth; and developing and fine-tuning the finishing details. Those who practice it at the very highest levels know how to heighten our experience of comfort through incremental adjustments: the turn of an arm, the choice of materials, the shaping of a silhouette or profile.

Like so much of design, comfort should be appropriate to the purpose. A desk chair is successful when it gives you a certain ergonomic support and maneuverability. The same is also true for a Charles of London chair, a design intended for use as a library reading chair. The arms on a Charles of London chair are thickly padded, so when you're reading the paper or a book, the cushions support and cradle your elbows; the calibrated outside pitch of the chair back holds you in a recumbent position, relaxed and reclined but not fully stretched out, a terrifically comfortable position for reading. A classic Turkish chair is extra deep, with a tight, sprung seat and the inside back and arms hand-tied and button-tufted: in its Edwardian way, this superbly comfortable design allows the occupant to relax with legs curled underneath and dream (the smell of citrus, sweet coffee, and jasmine in the air). Hence the name.

In a well-designed room, it shouldn't take you long to go from standing to seated. Comfort is finding yourself compelled to sit in a certain chair when you want to read, gravitating to a specific sofa when you

The settee was designed for practical comfort: it has an elliptical front, which is decidedly more comfortable than a straight edge.

entertain, selecting only one chair of twelve when you dine, or thinking only of your bed at home when you stay in a hotel. Should you find yourself nodding off on a great sofa, on the verge of a lovely little nap, chalk one up for comfort. Another victory for furniture!

"The house has to serve comfort. The work of art is revolutionary; the house is conservative." —ADOLF LOOS

I KNOW THAT ROOMS CAN SEDUCE US. SOME rooms wear their charms only on the surface, their beauty merely skin deep. Great rooms from highly skilled decorators always tempt, and they not only live up to their first impressions, but they also improve over time. One of the initial judgments we inevitably make about our rooms is whether they're comfortable or not. Ask yourself if your rooms give back the same level of pleasure with which they present themselves. Do they suit you in style and temperament? Do they actually fit you physically and emotionally? Are they as comfortable as they looked when they first seduced you?

Comfort is a wonderful luxury precisely because the decorator can micromanage it so completely. Great decorating is about creating rooms that look exceptionally smart and "behave" exceptionally well,

rooms that look wonderfully desirable to those peering in, enticing the owner through the door and across the threshold. More important, great decorating ensures that those smart, enticing, and alluring rooms surpass those flirtations and deliver the real luxuries of ease and pleasure.

If you have the luxury of building a house, or even of renovating an existing property, you'll begin to discover an entirely new level of possibilities when it comes to comfort. These are the options of site, and they are specific to you. Where on the property, for example, do you want to locate the pool? What direction do you want your bedroom to face? Do you prefer hallways to traverse the structure closer to the exterior window walls (as the Venetians do), or would you rather they be at the central core of the building? Where would you like your library or family room, and what other rooms should they be adjacent to? If you delight in using the breakfast room in the morning because that room is kissed by the morning sun, it's the simple fact that the room is oriented to face east and on the light-filled side of the house.

All of these choices affect the comfort of your house, because comfort doesn't occur on its own—we create it. It is key to all the luxuries we consider part of the life well-lived. You know it when you feel it, because comfort is the vindication that you've made sound decisions.

Here, comfort is all about scale: the wraparound sofa incorporates a chaise lounge. The children who live here wrestle each other to figure out who gets to sit there.

ABOVE: *Stacks of well-loved books cover the entrance hall's center table. Being met by your "friends" is a very comfortable way to arrive home.* OPPOSITE: *We inset narrow mercury-mirror panels into the white columns to lift and lighten the library.*

RIGHT: *To give a focus to the long expanse of this wall, we put curtains on the primary pair of French windows and left the others unadorned.* PAGES 202–3: *This living room is full of great craftsmanship, which I think makes it one of the most comfortable rooms in America. All of the upholstered pieces are made to measure, and the heading of the gossamer valance is smocked by hand.* PAGE 204: *The wonderful nineteenth-century French miniature portrait on the easel creates an enchanting and intimate tablescape.* PAGE 205: *The client's own collection of hard-stone frogs adds personality.*

RIGHT: *A grand bay window in an urban apartment has the allure of a winter garden. Comfort and structure are not mutually exclusive, as you can see in the tight seats and split backs of the chair and settee.* PAGE 208: *Loose cushions, soft materials, and forms designed to envelop and surround are the essential tools of comfort.* PAGE 209: *Remember this old adage: fifty cents for bread and fifty cents for flowers. Splurge on the blooms. They are as important as the furnishings.* PAGES 210–11: *I wanted this urban family room to have all the comforts of a ski lodge.*

RIGHT: *Instead of a low table, I used a big, tufted ottoman. It's a timely and flexible solution, and oftentimes it does a much better job.* FOLLOWING LEFT PAGE: *We created these chairs for, and with, the client, incorporating the back of one design with the arm of another. We call them the Leonard chair. Since we completed this house, he's ordered four more. Smart man.* FOLLOWING RIGHT PAGE: *These clients are comfortable with the trappings of family life.*

ABOVE AND OPPOSITE: *These unique slipcovers are made of an Italian-weave cotton seersucker. The sofa's French seams enhance the shape of the arm.*

*Instead of one large table,
we used these two small
wood versions so people
could get to and from the sofa
through the center.*

delight

CHOICE IS THE GREATEST OF ALL LUXURIES, SO WHY NOT OPT FOR DELIGHT? IN life and in décor, delight is the alpha and the omega. Where better to pursue happiness than home? Who better to help you discover it than a great decorator?

"The capacity for delight is the gift of paying attention."
—JULIA MARGARET CAMERON

THERE'S SOMETHING INHERENTLY DELIGHTFUL ABOUT CERTAIN ROOMS, OBJECTS, materials, and surfaces, although identifying and defining what that "something" is often proves elusive. We can recognize the little leap our heart takes at the sight of candlelight flickering in a window on a winter night, or the pleasurable sigh we breathe at a sublimely tapered, fluted leg on a Louis XVI settee, or the flight of glee we might experience at the discovery of a matte-painted Gustavian chest. We should know these feelings and revel in them. We should put ourselves in situations where they occur precisely because they give us pleasure.

Delight is that quality in design that transports us, that gives us cheer, that makes us smile and even laugh. Irreverence, wit, and whimsy can help fill a room with cheer so those who enter respond in kind. Great decorators know how to achieve that certain cheekiness. They understand how to recalibrate the atmosphere of an elegant, historically accurate interior with just the right top note—a visual

PREVIOUS PAGE: *The table is Italian inlay, with bronze and mother-of-pearl filigree, and it's absolutely marvelous!* OPPOSITE: *The eighteenth-century Russian commode, one of a pair, contributes handsomely to the architectural integrity of this Connecticut living room.*

trill, a flourish that not only punctuates the luxurious, staid room, but also transforms it with a bracing infusion of true individuality. Pleasures like that come from a sense of discovery and a confidence and comfort in your own perspective. To find that in decoration, as in people, is exhilarating and rare. Great rooms, houses, and gardens reveal the personalities of their owners—think of it as autobiography through design and decoration.

"The true delight is in the finding out rather than in the knowing." —ISAAC ASIMOV

THERE'S A STORY ABOUT THOMAS JEFFERSON at Monticello that illustrates another aspect of delight. Monticello was then, and remains today, an extraordinary exemplar of taste, refinement, and luxurious living. Jefferson designed Monticello to satisfy his own expansive sense of order and pleasure. But Jefferson, it turns out, also had a somewhat simpler side: he loved cool, freshly pressed sheets. When the sweltering Virginia nights woke him, he knew which of the other bedrooms had fresh sheets—say, the Blue Bedroom—and, knowing that those beds were cool, he'd wander through the darkness and slip into that room. Two hours later he'd awake again drenched; thinking of another place, perhaps the downstairs sleeping porch, he would go and slide into bed there. That's luxuriously delightful! It's as cool as the other side of the pillow and as simple as a freshly made bed.

Light and delight really do go hand in glove, especially when cut crystal, beading, or other embellishments are involved. Picture this: a Dr. Zhivagoesque expression of delirious magic in a glamorous urban environment. The stage is set by a pair of delicate, extravagantly beaded crystal chandeliers that shimmer as brilliantly as snow and ice in the sun. Each crystal tour de force hangs over one of two dining room tables. The morning after our client and her family moved in, I ask, "How was your first night? Did your family love having dinner under those gorgeous chandeliers?" She replied, "What dinner? I don't even remember what we ate! I spent the entire evening captivated by the sparkle of those chandeliers!"

Another client recently called complaining that she'd spent the first night in her newly decorated apartment and had a terrific backache! Perhaps the mattress we selected just wasn't comfortable enough, I thought. But honestly, we had test-driven everything in that apartment to make sure that, in addition to being luxurious, beautiful, and reflective of her personality, it was all deliciously comfortable. "How in the world," I asked, "could you possibly have a backache?" "Well," she replied, "I was so enthralled, so transported by that 1930s mercury-glass chandelier, I crawled up onto the dining room table and fell asleep, spent the entire night there, spread out like a corpse!" Talk about suffering for beauty.

There's great pleasure in collecting and using something that you love. This client adores jasp and that enhances the room's story.

"Intelligence is nothing without delight."
—PAUL CLAUDEL

WHEN DELIGHT FILLS A HOUSE, YOU CAN SENSE it at the door. It's in the scent of a Thanksgiving turkey roasting in the kitchen or the sound of children's laughter in the playroom. And it's something that the decorator tries to elicit with every decision, every detail, and every purchase. The simplest, most subtle choices can contribute to the overall effect, even if they do it subliminally: the way a painter has hand-brushed the walls, the way an upholsterer finished the arm of a chair, the gleam that the gilder has added to water-gilded surfaces, the burnished details on a japanned chest of drawers.

Our rooms, our houses, should be autobiographical in the best possible sense. The craft of the decorator helps us discover and express ourselves. The art of decoration helps others understand us better. The decoration of houses can encourage a family to grow and develop. It can also assist us in sharing the best of ourselves with others. Decoration is an investment in living, not necessarily in furnishings. The result of that investment should be pleasure and happiness—and, of course, delight.

I believe that delight is integral to the creation of memory, and to the family narrative. In creating our environments, we, by extension, build our lives as we would have them at their best and most optimistic. Our rooms become filled with memories, ever more so as time passes: our memories may be unspoken, or perhaps shared from one generation to the next through the objects we select and the stories of why we chose them, where they were found, and what they mean to us. Rooms, after all, are scrapbooks of a sort: our choices in decoration become mementos of all the opportunities that are offered us. That greater sense of possibility, of obligation, optimism, and delight, is a very American trait. And as far as I'm concerned, there's no better place for the pursuit of happiness than at home.

"Once we believe in ourselves, we can risk curiosity, wonder, spontaneous delight, or any experience that reveals the human spirit."
—E. E. CUMMINGS

OPPOSITE: *The joy of placing in the horse show is part of everyday life for this family, and the ribbon to prove it still gets pride of place.* FOLLOWING PAGES: *The 1930s mirrored ballroom fixture is one of a pair. We have a pin spot on it so it does what it was intended to do, or perhaps more!*

Delight is oftentimes a matter of reflection. This room would be only half as successful without the mirror over the sofa.

ABOVE AND OPPOSITE: *The way we light a room makes an enormous difference in how people feel in it. A combination of sconce light and a crystal chandelier does a fantastic job animating rooms.*

RIGHT: *This dining room was built specifically to accommodate twenty-four people at the table, because the members of this family regularly get together and celebrate with each other.* PAGES 236–37: *There's something so joyful about this type of abundance. What's more delightful than a cornucopia of roses, tulips, and fruit?* PAGES 238–39: *To really make the light dance around this room, we've used a pair of mirrors to reflect the chandeliers.*

Art is delight—this remarkable relief is by Jacob Hashimoto, a Japanese-American artist.

ABOVE: *This room is full of delicious materials to touch, from the hopsacking on the walls to the silk voided-velvet on the pillows to the linen velvet on the sofas.* OPPOSITE: *Color is the essence of delight. What could be more joyous than this Japanese red lacquer secretaire with its collection of chartreuse glazed vases?* FOLLOWING PAGES: *Truly luxurious—an indoor pool surrounded by plenty of ebonized wicker seating from Brenda Antin in Los Angeles.*

RIGHT: *I love dark-painted wicker, similar to that seen in Maine. The familiarity of the material and the finish give me great pleasure.*
FOLLOWING PAGES: *We designed this fireplace with Paul Lanier, the San Francisco artist, as a metaphor for sitting around a campfire.*

The bathtub in this bedroom,
with a view of Nantucket harbor,
is one of the most seductive
spots in this house.

We want to encourage creativity in children the way we do all other aspects of their intellectual development. Here, the crafts table in the center of the children's playroom entices them with the great pleasures of artistic expression.

I invited artist Nancy Lorenz to embellish this scenic wallpaper with gold-leaf calligraphy that captures the light and provides an irreverent take on a timeless pattern.

acknowledgments

THE HOUSES AND APARTMENTS IN THIS BOOK FOCUS ON SOME OF MY WORK OVER the past three years. Thanks to my clients, who have encouraged and inspired me, believed and trusted in what only I could see, and generously permitted me to record some of the highlights of their projects.

Thanks, too, to all of the architects, contractors, workrooms, craftspeople, and vendors who have encouraged and nurtured the success of my company over the past twenty-plus years.

Thanks, again, to my office staff, who have provided me with years of diligence, service, and the professional expertise that has helped me realize my projects from conception to completion.

Finally, kudos to my talented art director Doug Turshen and the gifted Judith Nasatir, both of whom helped articulate my message with creativity and flare.

First published in the United States in 2008 by
Rizzoli International Publications, Inc.
300 Park Avenue South
New York, NY 10010
www.rizzoliusa.com

2008 2009 2010 2011 / 10 9 8 7 6 5 4 3 2 1

ISBN 10: 0-8478-3054-3
ISBN 13: 978-0-8478-3054-1

Library of Congress Control Number: 200892667

Designed by Doug Turshen with David Huang

Printed in China